# -My Family-
# My Two Moms

by Claudia Harrington
illustrated by Zoe Persico

**Looking Glass Library**

An Imprint of Magic Wagon
abdopublishing.com

To Ken, Tess, Gretchen & Emmett - the best family ever! And to my extended SCBWI family, especially Lee Wind. Additional thanks to Emily Sylvan Kim. —CH

To my mom and dad for being the best parents in the world and supporting what I love to do. —ZP

abdopublishing.com

Printed in the United States of America, North Mankato, Minnesota.
052015
092015

THIS BOOK CONTAINS
RECYCLED MATERIALS

Written by Claudia Harrington
Illustrated by Zoe Persico
Edited by Heidi M.D. Elston
Designed by Candice Keimig

**Library of Congress Cataloging-in-Publication Data**

Harrington, Claudia, 1957- author.
  My two moms / by Claudia Harrington ; illustrated by Zoe Persico.
    pages cm. -- (My family)
  Summary: Lenny, the class reporter, follows Elsie for a school project and learns about her life with her two moms.
  ISBN 978-1-62402-110-7
1. Lesbian mothers--Juvenile fiction. 2. Mothers and daughters--Juvenile fiction. 3. Gay parents--Juvenile fiction. 4. Families--Juvenile fiction. [1. Lesbian mothers--Fiction. 2. Mothers and daughters--Fiction. 3. Gay parents--Fiction. 4. Family life--Fiction. 5. Youths' art.] I. Persico, Zoe, 1993- illustrator. II. Title.
  PZ7.1.H374My 2016
  [E]--dc23
                                    2015002676

On the day Lenny joined
Miss Fish's second grade
class, he had a camera
stuck to his face.

"It's for a project," said Lenny.

"But, Miss Fish!" cried the class. "Electronics are against the rules!"

"He's the class reporter," said Miss Fish. She winked at Lenny.

Miss Fish

When the bell rang,
Miss Fish took
Lenny aside.

"Remember, you're going to Elsie's house today. She's Student of the Week." **Click!**

"Do you take the bus?" asked Lenny.

Elsie knocked on Lenny's camera lens.

"Yes," she replied. "Do you have a dog?"

**Click!** Lenny popped his head out from behind the camera as they found two seats together. "How about if I ask the questions?" he said.

"Hi, Mom! Hi, Mommy! We're home!"
called Elsie as they burst through
the door. "Lenny, these are my moms.
And this is Wiggles."
"Welcome, Lenny," said Mom. **Click!**

"Make yourself at home," said Mommy. **Click!**

"Schoolwork first, then you two can play," called Mommy.

"We just have a spelling word search," said Elsie.

"Who helps with your homework?" asked Lenny. "I do my homework, silly," said Elsie. "But Mommy checks it. She helps if I get stuck. But I didn't!"

"Do you have a fish?" asked
Elsie.
Lenny sighed and followed
Elsie outside.

"Wiggles!" cried Elsie. "Quick! She's an inside cat!" **Click!**

"Who gets her down when she gets stuck in a tree?" asked Lenny.

"That would be me," said Mom, carrying a ladder. **Click!**

When Wiggles was safely inside,
Elsie showed Lenny her seesaw.
"Ow!" cried Elsie.

"Who gets your splinters out?" asked Lenny.

"Mommy's the best splinter getter-outer," sniffed Elsie.

"All done!" said Mommy, kissing Elsie's bandaged finger. **Click!**
"You're less wiggly than our new baby chimp at the zoo!"

"He's so cute," said Elsie. "Do you have a gerbil?"
Lenny shook his head.

"Who makes your dinner?"
asked Lenny.

"Mom builds the french fry skyscrapers, and we get to drizzle the ketchup to make them look cool." **Click!**

"Do you have a turtle?" asked Elsie.

"No turtle," said Lenny, smiling. "Who makes you brush your teeth?"

"I do that myself!" said Elsie. "Mom! Mommy! The handle came off again!" **Click!**

"Do you have a duck?" asked Elsie.

Lenny stepped over the bathroom river. "No, we move a lot."

"Who reads to you?" asked Lenny.

"Mommy and Mom both read to me. I'm an Elsie sandwich!"
**Click!**

"Last question," said Lenny, when his mother arrived. "Who loves you best?"

Mom and Mommy answered, "We do."

# Student of the Week

## Elsie

"Are you sure you don't have a duck?" asked Elsie.

"No, but I do have Meatloaf," said Lenny.

"Meatloaf?" asked Elsie.

*Chirp!*

"I speak cricket," said Lenny.

"Meatloaf says good night, Elsie. See you tomorrow!"